Published in 2013 by The Rosen Publishing Group, Inc.
29 East 21st Street, New York, NY 10010

Copyright © 2013 Weldon Owen Pty Ltd. Originally published in 2011 by Discovery Communications, LLC

Photo Credits: **KEY** tl=top left; tc=top center; tr=top right; cl=center left; c=center; cr=center right; bl=bottom left; bc=bottom center; br=bottom right; bg=background
CBCD = Corbis PhotoDisc; GMi = Gary Miller; HH = Hedgehog House; iS = istockphoto.com; JH = John Hyatt; NLA = National Library of Australia; RM = Robyn Mundy; RGS = Royal Geographic Society; SPRI = Scott Polar Research Institute; SLNSW = State Library of NSW; wiki = Wikipedia
front cover bg NLA; bl RGS; **1**c RGS; **2–3**tc RGS; **4–5**cl RGS; **6**c RGS; tc, tl, cl, bc, bl wiki; **6–7**bg iS; **8–9**bg NLA; **9**bc RGS; tr SLNSW; **10–11**bg NLA; **12**bc RGS; **13**bc NLA; tc RGS; **14**bl NLA; tr SPRI; **15**bg NLA; **16–17**bg RGS; **17**bc NLA; **18**bc RM; **19**bc, tc RGS; cr SLNSW; **20**bc, tr NLA; **21**bc JH; tc NLA; **22–23**bg JH; **23**br HH; tr NLA; **24**cl GMi; **25**bc RM; **26**tr RM; **27**bl, tc NLA; br GMi; **30**bg CBCD; br, c, tr iS; **32**bg NLA

All illustrations copyright Weldon Owen Pty Ltd

Weldon Owen Pty Ltd
Managing Director: Kay Scarlett
Creative Director: Sue Burk
Publisher: Helen Bateman
Senior Vice President, International Sales: Stuart Laurence
Vice President Sales North America: Ellen Towell
Administration Manager, International Sales: Kristine Ravn

Library of Congress Cataloging-in-Publication Data

Brasch, Nicolas.
 Ernest Shackleton's Antarctic expedition / by Nicolas Brasch.
    p. cm. — (Discovery education: sensational true stories)
 Includes index.
 ISBN 978-1-4777-0063-1 (library binding) — ISBN 978-1-4777-0111-9 (pbk.) —
 ISBN 978-1-4777-0112-6 (6-pack)
 1. Shackleton, Ernest Henry, Sir, 1874–1922—Juvenile literature. 2. Explorers—Great Britain—Biography—Juvenile literature. 3. Antarctica—Discovery and exploration—British—Juvenile literature. I. Title.
 G875.S5B73 2013
 919.89—dc23
                                        2012019589

Manufactured in the United States of America

CPSIA Compliance Information: Batch #W13PK2: For Further Information contact Rosen Publishing, New York, New York at 1-800-237-9932

SENSATIONAL TRUE STORIES

ERNEST SHACKLETON'S ANTARCTIC EXPEDITION

NICOLAS BRASCH

PowerKiDS press.
New York

Contents

The Antarctic 6

Setting Out 8

Trapped in the Ice 10

Winter Horror 12

Ocean Camp....................................14

Making for Land................................16

On Elephant Island 18

In Search of Help..............................20

Getting to South Georgia 22

Across the Mountains 24

Rescue 26

The Journey.....................................28

Plan Your Own Trip 30

Glossary..31

Index 32

Websites 32

ANTARCTIC EXPEDITIONS

Explorers include James Cook, who captained a ship across the Antarctic Circle, and Roald Amundsen, who led the first team to the South Pole.

James Cook
1772–1775

Charles Wilkes
1838–1842

Robert Falcon Scott
1901–1904

Ernest Shackleton
1907–1909

Roald Amundsen
1910–1911

Sir Douglas Mawson
1911–1914

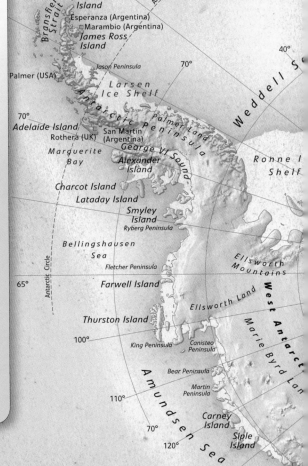

South Orkney Islands
(to UK)

Laurie Island
Orcadas (to Argentina)
Signy (to UK)

50°
60°
65°

60°

Antarctic Circle

Bransfield Strait

Joinville Island
Esperanza (Argentina)
Marambio (Argentina)
James Ross Island

Jason Peninsula

40°

70°

Palmer (USA)

Larsen Ice Shelf

Antarctic Peninsula

Palmer Land

Weddell S

70°

Adelaide Island
Rothera (UK)

San Martin (Argentina)

George VI Sound

Ronne I Shelf

Marguerite Bay

Alexander Island

Charcot Island
Lataday Island

Smyley Island
Ryberg Peninsula

Bellingshausen Sea

Fletcher Peninsula

Ellsworth Mountains

65°

Antarctic Circle

Farwell Island

Ellsworth Land

West Antarctica

Thurston Island

100°

King Peninsula

Canisteo Peninsula

Marie Byrd Lan

70°

Bear Peninsula

Amundsen Sea

Martin Peninsula

110°

Carney Island

120°

Siple Island

70°

Russkaya (Russia)

130°

140°

The Antarctic

Antarctica is the only continent on Earth where humans do not live permanently. Scientists visit and spend time there, but its climate and environment are too harsh for people. This is the reason why it is also the least explored continent. Despite this, the explorer Ernest Shackleton was fascinated by Antarctica. In 1914, he set off on an expedition, hoping to lead a team all the way across the continent.

Antarctica

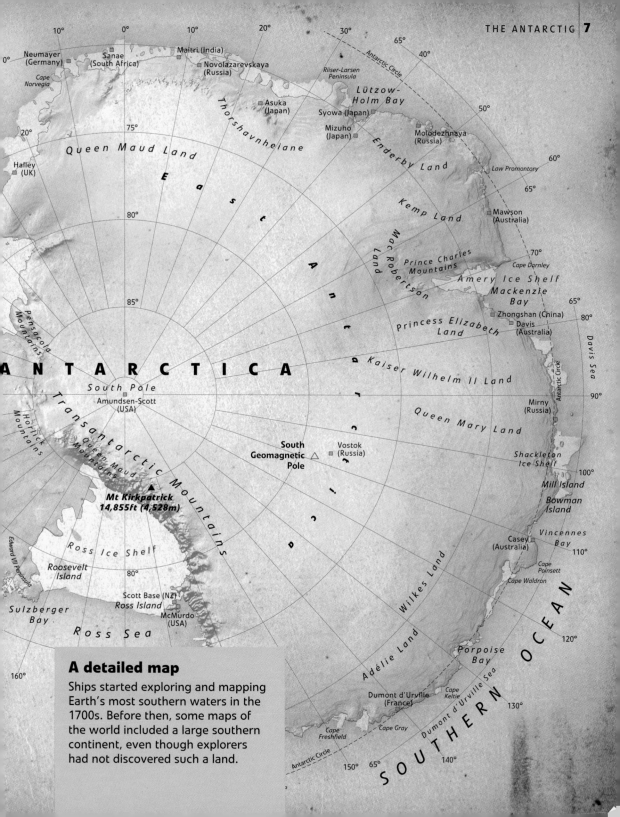

10°   0°   10°   20°   30°   65°   40°
0°
Neumayer   Sanae   Maitri (India)
(Germany)   (South Africa)   Novolazarevskaya
Cape   (Russia)   Riiser-Larsen   Antarctic Circle
Norvegia   Peninsula   50°
Lützow-
Asuka   Holm Bay
20°   (Japan)   Syowa (Japan)
75°   Mizuho   Molodezhnaya
Halley   (Japan)   (Russia)
(UK)   Enderby Land   60°
Queen Maud Land   Law Promontory
80°   E a s t   Kemp Land   65°
Mawson
(Australia)
70°
85°   Prince Charles   Cape Darnley
Mountains   Amery Ice Shelf
A   Mackenzie
Pensacola   Bay
Mountains   Princess Elizabeth   Zhongshan (China)   65°   80°
Land   Davis
n   (Australia)
A N T A R C T I C A   t   Kaiser Wilhelm II Land   90°
South Pole   a   Davis Sea
Amundsen-Scott   Queen Mary Land   Mirny
(USA)   (Russia)   Antarctic Circle
Horlick   c   Shackleton
Mountains   South   Vostok   Ice Shelf   100°
Geomagnetic   (Russia)
Pole   Mill Island
Mt Kirkpatrick   Bowman
14,855ft (4,528m)   Island
i   Vincennes
Casey   Bay
Ross Ice Shelf   (Australia)   110°
Roosevelt   80°   Cape
Island   a   Poinsett
Wilkes Land   Cape Waldron
Edward VII Peninsula   Scott Base (NZ)
Sulzberger   Ross Island   120°
Bay   McMurdo
(USA)   Porpoise
Ross Sea   Bay
160°   Adélie Land   SOUTHERN OCEAN
130°
A detailed map   Dumont d'Urville   Cape
(France)   Keltie
Ships started exploring and mapping   Dumont d'Urville Sea
Earth's most southern waters in the   Cape
1700s. Before then, some maps of   Freshfield   Cape Gray
the world included a large southern   Antarctic Circle   65°   140°
continent, even though explorers   150°
had not discovered such a land.

Thorshavnheiane
Mac. Robertson Land
Transantarctic Mountains
Queen Maud Mountains

Vahsel Bay
Shackleton planned to start the land crossing of Antarctica from Vahsel Bay. This bay was on the eastern shore of the Weddell Sea.

AUGUST 8, 1914
Setting Out

On August 8, 1914, the ship *Endurance* left from Plymouth, in England. After stopping in Buenos Aires, Argentina, it sailed to South Georgia, an island northwest of Antarctica. From there, Shackleton and the crew of the *Endurance* set off on what was known as the Imperial Trans-Antarctic Expedition. The expedition hit trouble almost immediately—and things only got worse. It would take a remarkable person to get everyone home safely.

Ernest Shackleton
Shackleton was born in 1874. In 1907–1909 he led his first Antarctic expedition, getting within 100 miles (160 km) of the South Pole

THE PLAN

Shackleton's plan was to land at Vahsel Bay, on the Antarctic coast, and trek across the continent, via the South Pole, to the Ross Sea on the other side. Here, he was to be met by a support party, which would bring food and supplies from Tasmania, Australia. Despite this being such a dangerous plan, more than 5,000 men applied to join the expedition.

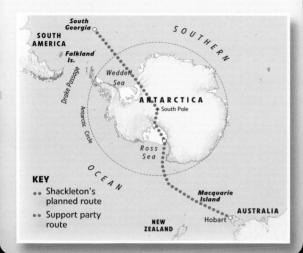

KEY

- Shackleton's planned route
- Support party route

Frank Hurley

Hurley, an Australian, was the expedition's photographer. He was a pioneer in photography. He took many black-and-white and some color photographs of the journey.

The *Endurance*

This three-masted ship with steam engines was made of wood. It weighed 392 tons (356 t) and was 144 feet (44 m) long. Its crew of 28 men included scientists.

DECEMBER 5, 1914

Trapped in the Ice

Before sailing from South Georgia, Shackleton was warned that the ice was thicker than normal and that it could stop his ship from reaching Vahsel Bay. Despite this, he set off on December 5, hoping for the best. Within a week, polar pack ice had stopped the *Endurance* for the first time. The ship's progress slowed as it encountered walls of ice over the next few weeks. It was soon clear to Shackleton that the ship might become stuck in the ice and they would all be trapped for the winter.

Finding a path

As the weather worsened with the approach of winter, Shackleton ordered some of the crew onto the ice with picks and other tools. They tried to hack through the ice to create a channel that the *Endurance* could sail through. Unfortunately, they failed.

Antarctic Summer

DECEMBER — Leaves port, enters pack ice

JANUARY — Ice surrounds ship

FEBRUARY — Ship stuck in ice

MARCH — Begins to drift north with pack ice

NOVEMBER

OCTOBER — Ship finally crushed

SEPTEMBER

AUGUST

JULY

JUNE

MAY

APRIL

Ship pressed on all sides, drifts helplessly

TIME LINE

The Weddell Sea began to freeze again at the end of the Antarctic summer, in late January and February. Sea ice can be as thick as 12 feet (3.7 m) in winter. Through the winter months, the trapped *Endurance* drifted in the ice pack. As the temperature rose in spring, the pack unlocked and tons of ice jostled the ship on all sides.

JANUARY 18, 1915
Winter Horror

Ice was not the only problem that Shackleton and his men faced. Strong currents and gales meant that they had no control over where the *Endurance* drifted. On January 18, 1915, they got within about a day's sailing of Vahsel Bay but could get no closer. The *Endurance* drifted some 800 miles (1,290 km) north before getting stuck in the Weddell Sea ice pack. In the long winter, they were at the mercy of the drifting mass of ice and the freezing temperatures. They could not land on Antarctica, nor sail back to South America.

Standing on the stirring ice one can imagine it is disturbed by the breathing and tossing of a mighty giant below.

ERNEST SHACKLETON

Staying motivated
Shackleton let his men play soccer and hockey on the ice around the ship. This kept them fit and warm and helped lift their morale.

As well as men to sail and repair the ship, the crew included engineers, doctors, and an artist.

Caring for the sled dogs
There were dogs on board, which were to be used to pull the sleds on the land crossing of Antarctica. The men cared for them and caught penguins and seals to feed to them.

Dog kennels
During the height of winter, the crew set up camp on the ice. They built shelters similar to igloos for their sled dogs and called these shelters dogloos.

OCTOBER 27, 1915
Ocean Camp

In October 1915, the ice began to crush the *Endurance*. The men tried to make repairs as different parts of the ship cracked apart and started to leak. On October 27, Shackleton ordered everyone off the ship. They took lifeboats, sleds, food, tools, and as many provisions as they could carry. They set up Ocean Camp on an ice floe. Within a month, the *Endurance* had broken up and sunk.

SHIP'S ANIMALS

Fresh meat was very scarce. Shackleton ordered that only the sled dogs could continue with the expedition. The ship's cat and the sled puppies could not be allowed to survive.

> ❚❚ *We have been compelled to abandon the ship, which is crushed beyond all hope of ever being righted.* ❚❚
>
> **ERNEST SHACKLETON**

Survival
Shackleton (right) and Frank Hurley sit beside a stove at Ocean Camp. To conserve their food supplies, the men cooked seal or penguin stew whenever possible. They also used the blubber as a fuel for their stoves.

A long way to land
When the *Endurance* was crushed in the ice and then started sinking, the men were still 200 nautical miles (370 km) from the nearest land. They had to deal with the ice melting and drifting.

DECEMBER 20, 1915
Making for Land

By December 1915, with the approach of the Antarctic summer, the melting ice had started to break up. Shackleton realized that he and his men would have to start trekking toward the nearest land. On December 20, they set off, sinking in the soft snow and struggling with the weight of the provisions, as well as the three lifeboats, which they had to drag across the ice floes. They headed northwest.

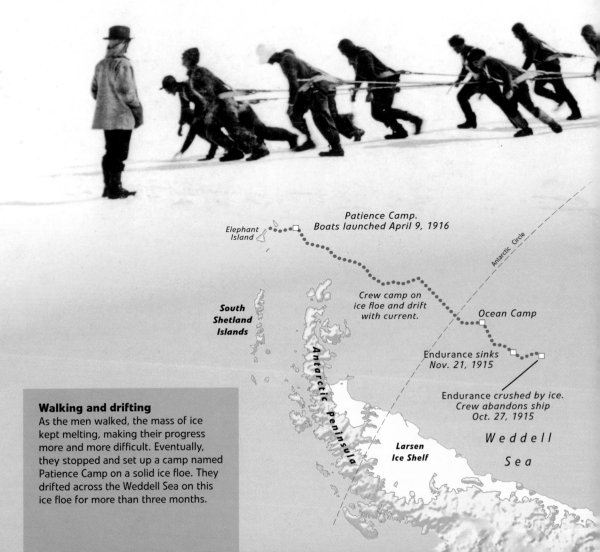

Patience Camp.
Boats launched April 9, 1916

Elephant
Island

Antarctic Circle

South
Shetland
Islands

Crew camp on
ice floe and drift
with current.

Ocean Camp

Endurance sinks
Nov. 21, 1915

Endurance crushed by ice.
Crew abandons ship
Oct. 27, 1915

Antarctic Peninsula

Larsen
Ice Shelf

W e d d e l l

S e a

Walking and drifting
As the men walked, the mass of ice kept melting, making their progress more and more difficult. Eventually, they stopped and set up a camp named Patience Camp on a solid ice floe. They drifted across the Weddell Sea on this ice floe for more than three months.

Lifeboat on ice

Pulling and pushing the lifeboats across the ice was a slow and exhausting task. The boats, filled with the remaining provisions, were placed on wooden planks that acted like sleds. Some men in harnesses pulled while other men pushed.

Breaking up Patience Camp

When the ice floe holding the camp broke up, the men took to the boats and rowed. The boats were often caught between ice floes and had to be pulled free.

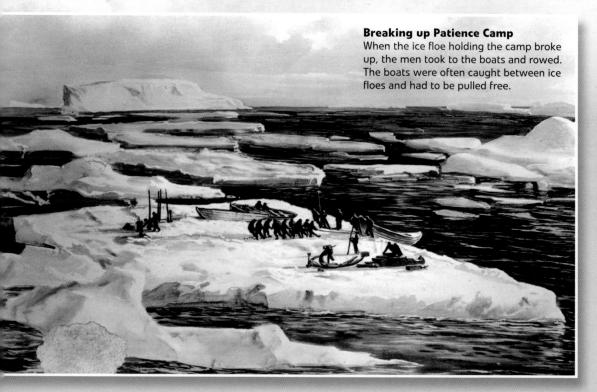

APRIL 12, 1916
On Elephant Island

On April 12, 1916, Shackleton and his men spotted Elephant Island from their lifeboats. This isolated, mountainous piece of rock and ice off the coast of Antarctica was not the land that they had been heading toward. But exhausted, they put their lifeboats ashore. It was 497 days since they had last set foot on land. It took them several days to find a good camping spot because Elephant Island provided almost no shelter from the icy gales, blizzards, and crashing waves.

Remote location
Elephant Island was too remote for whaling ships or other ships to pass by and rescue the men. Shackleton needed to find a way to get them off the island.

On land at last
The men dragged the boats ashore. Some collapsed from exhaustion. Some could not stand because their feet were numb with frostbite.

Notebook entry
This notebook shows how the lifeboats were used for sleeping. Each man was allocated his own sleeping position inside a boat.

Hut from a lifeboat
To escape the wind, ice, and waves, the men slept inside the upturned boats. They strapped canvas sails over the boats to stop water from leaking in.

APRIL 24, 1916

In Search of Help

S hackleton spent several days deciding what to do. His choices were limited because the direction of the winds made it impossible to sail to some of the closer destinations. He decided to leave 22 men on Elephant Island and sail with five men for the whaling station on the island of South Georgia. It was 800 miles (1,300 km) away. Provisions were loaded onto the lifeboat the *James Caird*, and the six men set off on April 24.

Frank Worsley
This experienced sea captain was in charge of navigating the *James Caird* across the ocean to South Georgia.

Setting off
An 800-mile-(1,300 km) trip through the freezing, stormy Southern Ocean on a small, weather-beaten lifeboat was madness. But Shackleton had no choice.

Farewell
The remaining men knew it might be the last time they saw Shackleton and the five men. They also knew that if the *James Caird* did not get to South Georgia, they would likely never be rescued.

THE *JAMES CAIRD*

The *James Caird* was just 22.5 feet (6.9 m) long, but it was heavier and stronger than the other two lifeboats. On Elephant Island it was specially modified for the journey and loaded with enough provisions to last a four-week trip.

Ballast
The boat's ballast was made of blankets filled with sand.

Masts and sails
Masts were fitted so the boat could sail when winds were right.

Deck
A deck was built using wood and canvas and fitted to the boat.

JAMES CAIRD

MAY 10, 1916
Getting to South Georgia

Huge waves, bitter winds, little sunlight, and icy water that froze to the side of the boat made the trip a nightmare. The men's clothes were wet from the start and never had a chance to dry out. The smallest error in navigation by Frank Worsley would mean that they would miss South Georgia completely and die at sea. But somehow, they made it. Two days after sighting South Georgia, they managed to land on the island on May 10.

Enormous wave
At one point during a storm, Shackleton thought the sky was clearing. Then he realized, "what I had seen was not a rift in the clouds but the white crest of an enormous wave."

Land at last
Because of rough seas and big winds, it took the men two days to find a safe place to land and drag the boat ashore.

On South Georgia
In their first days on the island, the men killed baby albatross and seals for food. They rested and got their strength back.

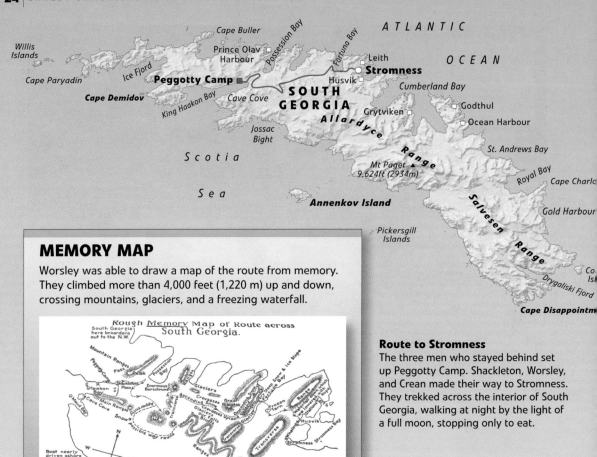

ATLANTIC

OCEAN

Willis Islands

Cape Buller

Possession Bay

Prince Olav Harbour

Fortuna Bay

Leith

Stromness

Cape Paryadin

Ice Fjord

Peggotty Camp ■

Husvik

Cumberland Bay

Cape Demidov

Cave Cove

King Haakon Bay

SOUTH GEORGIA

Grytviken

Godthul

Ocean Harbour

Allardyce

Jossac Bight

Range

St. Andrews Bay

Scotia

Mt Paget ▲
9,624ft (2934m)

Royal Bay

Cape Charlo

Sea

Annenkov Island

Salvesen

Gold Harbour

Pickersgill Islands

Range

Drygalski Fjord

Co Is

Cape Disappointm

MEMORY MAP

Worsley was able to draw a map of the route from memory. They climbed more than 4,000 feet (1,220 m) up and down, crossing mountains, glaciers, and a freezing waterfall.

Route to Stromness

The three men who stayed behind set up Peggotty Camp. Shackleton, Worsley, and Crean made their way to Stromness. They trekked across the interior of South Georgia, walking at night by the light of a full moon, stopping only to eat.

MAY 15, 1916

Across the Mountains

The men had landed on the northwest coast of South Georgia. Unfortunately, the whaling station at Stromness was on the northeast side. Shackleton felt that the *James Caird* was not fit to sail around the coastline. Instead, he decided that three men would trek across the South Georgia mountains while the other three would remain behind and wait to be rescued. Shackleton, Worsley, and Tom Crean set off on May 15.

Sliding down mountains
The men coiled their rope into a type of sled, sat on it, and slid down the slippery ice of steep mountainsides.

Arriving in Stromness
Norwegian whalers working at Stromness welcomed the exhausted men and gave them hot baths, haircuts, clean clothes, and an enormous meal.

AUGUST 30, 1916
Rescue

Worsley and some whalers sailed to Peggotty Camp and returned with Timothy McCarthy, John Vincent, and Henry McNish. Shackleton would not rest. Instead, he made preparations to reach the men still on Elephant Island. The day after the Peggotty Camp rescue, he, Worsley, and Crean set off on the *Southern Sky,* but failed. On the fourth attempt, this time in the *Yelcho*, they succeeded in landing on August 30.

Point Wild
The 22 men on Elephant Island were campe[d] at Point Wild. It was constantly hit by huge waves from ice breaking off nearby glacier[s]

Barrier of ice
The *Southern Sky* was stopped by pack ice 60 miles (95 km) from Elephant Island. Another three rescue attempts had to be made.

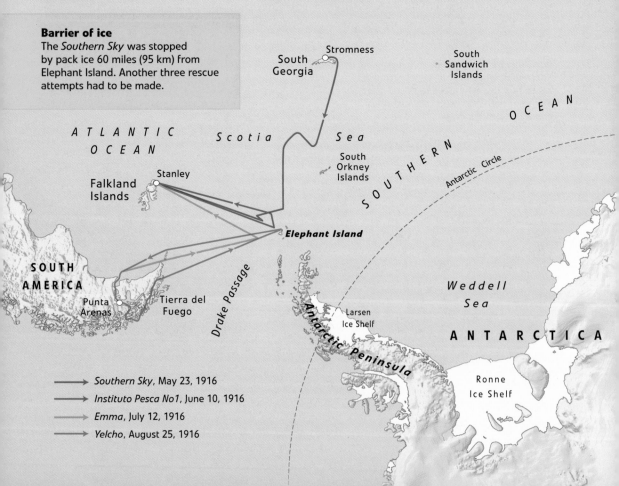

Stromness

South Georgia

South Sandwich Islands

ATLANTIC OCEAN

Scotia   Sea

OCEAN

South Orkney Islands

SOUTHERN

Antarctic Circle

Stanley

Falkland Islands

Elephant Island

SOUTH AMERICA

Punta Arenas

Tierra del Fuego

Drake Passage

Weddell Sea

Antarctic Peninsula

Larsen Ice Shelf

ANTARCTICA

Ronne Ice Shelf

→ *Southern Sky*, May 23, 1916
→ *Instituto Pesca No1*, June 10, 1916
→ *Emma*, July 12, 1916
→ *Yelcho*, August 25, 1916

Left behind
For four months, 22 men survived on one of the most isolated places on Earth. One man is missing from the photo—recovering after having his frostbitten toes amputated.

The *Yelcho*
The small steam tug made it through the ice and landed on Elephant Island. The survivors were taken on board and sailed immediately for Punta Arenas, in Chile. There, a huge crowd greeted them.

Memorial
This memorial on Elephant Island honors the expedition survivors and their rescuers. The statue is of Luis Pardo Villalón, captain of the *Yelcho*.

A T L A N

O C E A

Stanley

Falkland
Islands

Scotia

Sea

SOUTH

AMERICA

**Tierra del
Fuego**

Punta
Arenas

D r a k e   P a s s a g e

P

Elephant Island
Yelcho *rescues crew*
August 30, 1916

**South
Shetland
Islands**

KEY TO ROUTES

——— *Endurance*

·············· Ice drift

– – – – – *James Caird*

——— *Yelcho* rescue ship

A n t a r c t i c

Larse
Ice Sh

Antarctic Circle

A n t a r c t i c   P e

The Journey

The 28 men who set out on the *Endurance* were stranded
in Antarctic waters for more than 20 months. During
that time, they suffered from frostbite and other health
problems, faced horrific weather conditions, and feared for
their lives. They were stranded on their ship in the ice pack,
then watched it sink. They sailed through ice that smashed
against the sides of their lifeboats. They trekked across ice
floes that melted beneath their feet, and often ran short of
food. Yet, amazingly, all of them survived.

A N

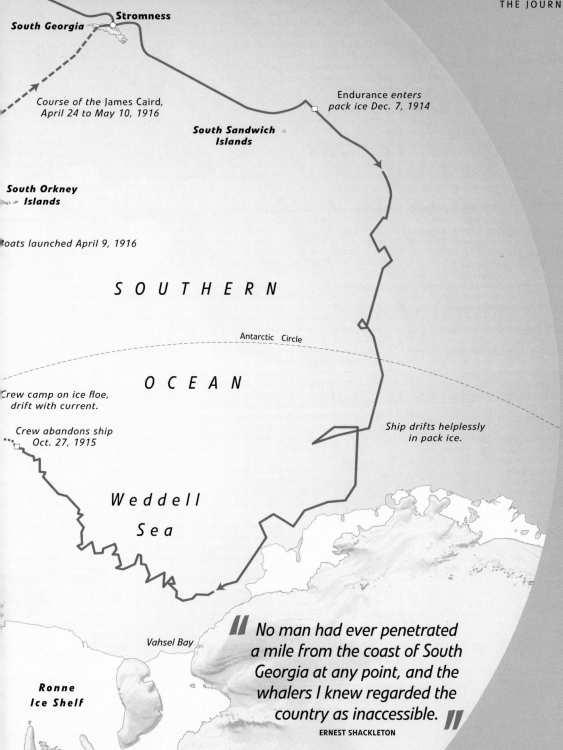

From
Buenos Aires

Stromness

South Georgia

Course of the James Caird,
April 24 to May 10, 1916

Endurance *enters*
pack ice Dec. 7, 1914

South Sandwich
Islands

South Orkney
Islands

Boats launched April 9, 1916

S O U T H E R N

Antarctic   Circle

O C E A N

Crew camp on ice floe,
drift with current.

Crew abandons ship
Oct. 27, 1915

Ship drifts helplessly
in pack ice.

W e d d e l l

S e a

Vahsel Bay

▌▌ No man had ever penetrated
a mile from the coast of South
Georgia at any point, and the
whalers I knew regarded the
country as inaccessible. **▌▌**
ERNEST SHACKLETON

Ronne
Ice Shelf

C T I C A

Plan Your Own Trip

A trip like the *Endurance* expedition needs to be well planned. Shackleton could not guarantee he could find new sources of food. To give you an idea of what is involved, it is your turn to plan a 20-month trip.

Pretend that you and five friends are going somewhere very isolated. Write down what you would take with you and how much of each item.

Don't forget to include:

1 Food

2 Water

3 Clothes

4 Tools

5 Medical supplies

and anything else you can think of.

Glossary

albatross (AL-buh-tros) A type of large seabird.

ballast (BA-luhst) Heavy material placed in the bottom of a boat to keep stable.

blizzard (BLIH-zurd) A very harsh snowstorm.

channel (CHA-nul) A route or path in the sea.

coiled (KOYLD) Wound into a circular shape.

frostbite (FROST-byt) A condition caused by extreme cold that causes serious damage to exposed parts of the body, particularly feet and hands.

harnesses (HAR-nes-ez) Gear that is tied to animals or people to help them pull heavy equipment.

ice floe (EYES FLOH) A sheet of floating ice that has broken off from a larger ice mass.

igloo (IH-gloo) A shelter made from ice.

inaccessible (ih-nik-SEH-suh-bul) Unable to be reached.

isolated (EYE-suh-lay-ted) On its own.

modified (MAH-dih-fyd) Altered or changed.

morale (muh-RAL) The mental and emotional feeling of a person or a group about the task at hand.

nautical (NAW-tih-kul) Having to do with ships or sailors.

penetrated (PEH-nuh-trayt-ed) Entered.

pick (PIK) A tool with a sharp end for digging and making holes.

provisions (pruh-VIH-zhunz) Food, equipment, and other supplies required on an expedition.

trek (TREHK) To explore on foot.

Index

A
Amundsen, Roald 6

C
Cook, James 6
Crean, Tom 24, 26

D
dogs 13, 14

E
Elephant Island 18, 19, 20, 21, 26, 27, 28
Endurance 8, 9, 10, 12, 14, 15, 28, 30

H
Hurley, Frank 9, 14

I
Imperial Trans-Antarctic Expedition 8

J
James Caird 20, 21, 28

M
Mawson, Douglas 6
McNish, Henry 26

O
Ocean Camp 14

P
Patience Camp 16, 17, 28
Peggotty Camp 24, 26
Point Wild 26

S
Scott, Robert Falcon 6
South Georgia 8, 10, 20, 22, 23, 24, 25, 29
Southern Sky 26
Stromness 24, 25, 29

V
Vahsel Bay 8, 9, 10, 12
Villalón, Luis Pardo 27
Vincent, John 26

W
Weddell Sea 8, 11, 12, 16, 29
Wilkes, Charles 6

Y
Yelcho 26, 27, 28

Websites

Due to the changing nature of Internet links, PowerKids Press has developed an online list of websites related to the subject of this book. This site is updated regularly. Please use this link to access the list: www.powerkidslinks.com/disc/antar/